The Ultimate MINISTRY TOOL BOX SERIES

D1059988

How to Raise Money for Your Ministry

Daniel King

How to Raise Money for Your Ministry

ISBN: 1-931810-14-1

Copyright: 2010
Daniel King
King Ministries International
PO Box 701113
Tulsa, OK 74170 USA
1-877-431-4276
daniel@kingministries.com
www.kingministries.com

Table of Contents

Introduction

Have you ever wanted to do something for God but were unable to because of lack of money? Maybe the Lord spoke to you about taking a mission trip to a certain country, but as much as your heart cried to go, you were unable to purchase a plane ticket because you had no extra funds. Perhaps your church is outgrowing its current facility and is in need of a new building, but due to insufficient finances, your church can't afford a larger facility. All those people your heart longs to reach for the Kingdom seem just out of reach – all because of a lack of money.

Ministry requires money. T.L. Osborn said, "Without money you have no ministry." He told me, "If you can't raise money, you won't last long in the ministry." Many people have big visions, many are kind hearted, but ultimately a ministry must have money to survive. The Gospel is free, but it takes a lot of money to communicate the good news.

You need money:

To rent a sound system.

To mail a letter.

To purchase a plane ticket.

To publish a book.

To build a church.

To feed the hungry.

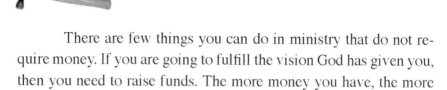
There are few things you can do in ministry that do not require money. If you are going to fulfill the vision God has given you, then you need to raise funds. The more money you have, the more people you will be able to reach for the Kingdom of God.

Imagine wanting to feed a starving child but finding that your pocket is empty. See yourself standing in front of a large crowd but being unable to communicate because you have no sound system. Visualize trying to get on an airplane with no plane ticket. Each of these problems can be solved with a little bit of money. Ecclesiastes 10:19 tells us, *"Money answers everything."* Money helps you solve problems, meet people's needs, and preach the Gospel.

Raising money is vital to fulfilling the vision of your ministry. Throughout modern church history, every great minister became a great fundraiser. They became masters at inspiring people to give toward their vision.

Today, more ministries fail because of lack of money than for any other reason. I know many people who want to be missionaries, but because they are up to their eyeballs in debt, they will never be free to go to the mission field. There are a thousand preachers who would like to preach at crusades, but only a handful of crusade evangelists. Why? Because most are unable to raise the money necessary to do crusades.

In this book, I want to share with you ten secrets to help you raise funds for your ministry. As you prayerfully apply these principles, I believe the necessary finances will begin flowing into your ministry. You have a job to do for the Kingdom, and Heaven has all the resources needed for you to fulfill your mission!

Chapter 1

Boldness

Do you ever feel "yuck" when you try to raise money? Once, I invited a friend to go with me on a mission trip. I encouraged him to send a letter to all his friends and relatives asking them to help with the cost of the trip. However, my friend was uncomfortable asking other people for money because it made him feel like a beggar. Because of his reluctance, he never mailed any letters, never raised any money, and never went with me on a mission trip.

His attitude is not uncommon. From an early age, we are taught to be self-sufficient, self-reliant, to make our own way in the world, and to never ask others for help. However, if you are truly going to be effective in ministry, you need to change your hesitant attitude and develop a boldness when asking people for money.

Fundraising is perhaps the most difficult part of ministry. D.L. Moody said, "Blessed are the fundraisers for in heaven they shall sit next to the martyrs." One missionary lamented that he was more worried about raising money than he was about being martyred on the mission field.

The truth is that if God has given you a *vision*, He has also called other people alongside you to help you with *provision*. Don't be ashamed of your message or your calling.

David Shibley, a premier missiologist, explained that in the beginning stages of ministry, he felt like he was wearing two hats. The first was his ministry hat that he loved. The second was a fundraising hat that he hated. A ministry consultant told him that the hats were actually the same hat, because without the fundraising, there would be no ministry. David explained he now feels it is an honor to ask people for money to help him reach the world for Jesus.

Your motive for fundraising should be to fulfill what God has called you to do. You should consider it a privilege to ask for money to help save the lost. You are not asking for yourself. You are asking for eternity. As a minister, when you ask for money, you are not asking for money to meet your own needs, you are asking on the behalf of others who have no voice. All you are is a conduit for God's blessing to flow from one person to a needy person.

Get over being uncomfortable asking people for money. Don't worry about what people think. Overcome your fears.

One day I received this letter in response to one of my fundraising e-mails:

Hello, I received your email about your ministry. I never heard of your ministry and have never asked to be contacted by your ministry. Don't send me any more emails asking for money. Remember what Jesus did to the moneychangers in the temple...I'm sure you have an understanding of the faith God asks us to have in Him to provide for our needs. You should try having faith in God for your finances instead of sending out unsolicited emails to people asking for money. Thank you for taking me off your email list and please represent the kingdom of God with more discretion and respect for our heavenly Father.

This man's angry words did not bother me. Why? Because in response to the same fundraising email, I received a donation for $5000. Not everyone is called to support me, but it is my responsibility to find those who are called to help me lead people to Jesus.

James 4:2 explains, *"You do not have because you do not ask."* Jesus said, *"Ask and it will be given to you; seek and you will find; knock and the door will be opened to you. For everyone who asks receives; he who seeks finds; and to him who knocks, the door will be opened"* (Matthew 7:7-8 NIV). Often ministers have not been able to raise money because they have not been bold enough to ask people to give.

According to *People Raising* by William P. Dillon, there are three approaches to raising money. The first was used by George Mueller who had an orphanage in England in the 1800's. He never shared his needs with anyone and simply trusted God to provide. He committed to live by faith. One day he did not have any food to feed his orphans. He asked them all to sit down at the kitchen table. As they bowed their heads to pray, there was a knock at the door. Sitting on the doorstep was a basket of food prepared with just enough food for all the orphans to eat. Throughout his ministry, Mueller never shared his needs and never sent out a newsletter asking for money, yet every time he faced a crisis, God supernaturally sent someone to help with the need.

Hudson Taylor, a missionary to China, used a second method. He shared his needs with people but never directly asked them for help. He believed in sharing information but not in direct solicitation.

Another great man of God was D.L. Moody of Chicago, Illinois. Moody was known as an aggressive fundraiser. He would often walk into the offices of local businessmen and ask for their help. Frequently he walked out with a large check. In the Billy Graham Museum at Wheaton College there hangs one of his fundraising letters that he mailed out to Sunday schools across America asking for donations. Moody was forceful and persistent in asking people for money to help fund his ministry outreaches. He actively shared information about the ministry's needs and he aggressively solicited people for funds.

Personally, I like to use D.L. Moody's method. There is nothing wrong with what George Mueller and Hudson Taylor did, but I believe the bolder you are in asking for money, the more people are inspired to give. No one method is right or wrong. Each minister must ask God for direction concerning which method to use in raising money. If any of my statements about fundraising in this book seem too aggressive, then feel free to develop your own style of raising money. God will honor your faith no matter which method you decide to follow.

It is Biblical for God's people to support God's workers.

1. God instructed the Israelites to support the tribe that was called to minister. *"Behold, I have given the children of Levi all the tithes in Israel as an inheritance in return for the work which they perform, the work of the tabernacle of meeting"* (Numbers 18:21).

2. Elijah asked the widow of Zarephath to sow a significant seed into his life (1 Kings 17:8-16).

3. Jesus was supported by His followers. *"Now it came to pass, afterward, that He went through every city and village, preaching and bringing the glad tidings of the kingdom of God. And the twelve were with Him, and certain women who had been healed of evil spirits and infirmities Mary called Magdalene, out of whom had come seven demons, and Joanna the wife of Chuza, Herod's steward, and Susanna, and many others who provided for Him from their substance"* (Luke 8:1-3).

4. Jesus told the Twelve to trust God for supporters as they preached. *"Provide neither gold nor silver nor copper in your money belts, nor bag for your journey, nor two tunics, nor sandals, nor staffs; for a worker is worthy of his food. Now whatever city or town you enter, inquire who in it is worthy, and stay there till you go out"* (Matthew 10:9-11).

5. Paul asked the Roman church to assist him with his mission trip to Spain (Romans 15:24).

6. Paul asked the Corinthian church for support as he headed toward Judea (2 Corinthians 1:15-16). I suggest you do an in-depth study of 2 Corinthians chapters eight and nine in order to see how aggressively Paul asked for money.

7. Paul thanked the Philippian church for supporting him even when no other church was helping him. *"I am full, having received from Epaphroditus the things sent from you, a sweet-smelling aroma, an acceptable sacrifice, well pleasing to God. And my God shall supply all your need according to His riches in glory by Christ Jesus"* (Philippians 4:18-19).

Chapter 2

Source

God is your source. Do not look to people for your funding; look to God. That way, when an individual does not give, you will not be disappointed. God will bring people alongside you to support you, but never look to people as the source of your funding. Anytime I start looking at a particular person for support, I am inevitably disappointed. But when I trust God for provision, He always supplies my needs, often in surprising ways.

No one owes you anything but love. Put your faith in God, not in any individual. The book of Hebrews instructs, *"Let us fix our eyes on Jesus, the author and perfecter of our faith"* (Hebrews 12:2 NIV).

My parents became missionaries to Mexico when I was ten years old. They left for the mission field without a regular paycheck, without any outside source of income, and with only a handful of people who supported them. I saw them trust God every month for money to buy food for our family. Yet not once did we go hungry.

We saw God provide on many occasions. One day my parents only had five dollars. They decided to use half of it to buy a gallon of milk and they sowed the other $2.50 into another ministry. Later that day, a friend slipped them an envelope with a $2,000 check.

As a teenager, I started believing God for money to go on mission trips. The first mission trip I ever took required $500. For me, that

amount seemed impossible. But God supernaturally provided. My next trip cost $1,200. Again, God provided. Now I regularly trust God for tens of thousands of dollars for our crusades.

The Psalmist observed, *"I have been young, and now am old; Yet I have not seen the righteous forsaken, Nor his descendants begging bread"* (Psalm 37:25).

God's will is God's bill. Hudson Taylor said, "God's work done God's way will never lack God's supply." God has abundant resources, and He is your Provider.

As you trust God for provision, here are some Scriptures that will build your faith:

* *"But as for me, I trust in You, O Lord; I say, 'You are my God.'"* (Psalm 31:14).

* *"It is better to trust in the Lord than to put confidence in princes"* (Psalm 118:9).

* *"But he who trusts in the Lord will be prospered"* (Proverbs 28:25).

* *"Blessed is the man who trusts in the Lord, and whose hope is the Lord"* (Jeremiah 17:7).

Chapter 3

Relationships

Everything in ministry rises and falls on relationships. According to Betty Barnett in her book *Friend Raising*, it is better to focus more on being a friend-raiser than on being a fundraiser. If you focus on building relationships, not only will your fundraising efforts be more successful, but you will also have people's hearts invested into your vision.

Fundraising should begin with those whom you know best like your family, close friends, and your home church. The more personal your fundraising efforts are, the more effective they will be. People like to give to those whom they know, care for, and trust.

1. Realize every relationship is important. When Jesus walked on this earth, He made relationships His top priority. Jesus was a people person, and I want to be a people person just like Him. I work hard to sustain my relationships and to form new ones. When I meet someone, I often ask for his email address or request a business card. I continually add people to my mailing list and email list. You never know when one of these contacts may become a regular partner with your ministry.

2. Paddle your canoe in many different waters. When I first started my ministry, I joined a small ministry fellowship. I traveled and preached at many of the churches in the fellowship, but one day

I realized that I would never be able to accomplish everything God has called me to do if I limited myself to one fellowship. I began to attend a variety of conferences and joined several different organizations. The more circles you are part of, the more successful your ministry will be.

3. Never burn bridges. One of my friends was a youth pastor at a denominational church. When he decided to launch out into full-time evangelistic ministry, he asked me if he should cut ties with his denomination. I encouraged him to remain connected to the denomination as much as possible. Now, most of the churches he preaches in belong to that group of churches.

Because people are unique and irreplaceable, it's important to value your relationships. Maintaining current relationships is always easier than building completely new ones. Although relationships take time to cultivate, well-established and nurtured relationships can become one of your greatest treasures.

4. Give your important relationships a personal touch. Sometimes when ministries grow big, their fundraising efforts start to look like mass marketing. However, the more personal you can be in your interaction with your partners, the better. Take the time to handwrite a thank you letter, make a phone call, send a postcard, or invite people over to your home for dinner. By going the extra mile, you will turn contacts into contributors, and partners will become close friends that will stick with you for life.

Treat your donors like you treat your best friends. Send them birthday, Christmas, and anniversary cards. Send pictures of your family and reports about what you are doing. Mail small gifts of appreciation. Remember what is important to them. Invite them to

come visit you on the mission field. Pray for them. Recall the names of their children.

5. Teamwork makes the dream work. One of my greatest secrets to fundraising is to involve others in the fundraising effort. In one of my first crusades in Panama, there were multiple ministers who shared the budget. My co-evangelist raised part of the money, a children's minister paid for the kids' outreach, a youth pastor contributed to the youth concert, some ladies helped with the cost of the women's conference, and a pastor gave towards the leadership conference. By myself, I did not have the full budget, but by working together, we were able to shake a city. T.E.A.M. means Together Everyone Achieves Miracles.

6. Use meal times to build your relationships with others. Keith Ferrazzi wrote a great book, *Never Eat Alone.* Invite people to your house for dinner. Take people out to lunch. A face-to-face personal meeting is probably the best way to build relationships. Even John the Apostle knew that meeting with people was better than writing a letter. He wrote to the Church, *"Having many things to write to you, I did not wish to do so with paper and ink; but I hope to come to you and speak face to face, that our joy may be full"* (2 John 1:12).

7. People desire to have a two-way conversation with you. Make a way for that to happen. It is just as important to listen to others as it is to talk. Provide a way for people to share their prayer requests and testimonies with you. Care about people as individuals.

Chapter 4

Vision

Vision drives fundraising, not need. People do not give to need; they give to vision. If you want to raise money, you must have a clear, focused vision. What are you called to do? Whom are you going to reach? If I give you money, what will you do with it?

When I was fifteen years old, I was reading a book about how to be successful. The book said that young people should write down their goals. One of the goals this book mentioned was for young people to try to become a millionaire by the age of thirty. Because of my upbringing as a missionary in Mexico, I realized that money is not important to me, but rather souls. I wrote down this goal, "I, Daniel King, want to lead one million people to Jesus before I turn thirty years of age." This goal became my vision. Every time I spoke, I talked about the vision of leading a million people to Jesus. I became known for my passion for soulwinning. People started to support me because they knew my vision was to lead people to Jesus. Before I turned thirty, I completed the goal. Now, my vision is to lead one million souls to Christ every year.

Here are a few key principles to keep in mind about vision:

1. A ministry without vision will fail. The Bible says, *"Where there is no vision, the people perish"* (Proverbs 29:18 KJV). If you aim at nothing, you will hit it every time. You must have a plan. If you fail to plan, you plan to fail. Proverbs 21:5 says, *"The plans of the*

diligent lead surely to plenty, but those of everyone who is hasty, surely to poverty."

2. Your vision must be written down. Habakkuk 2:2-3 states, *"Then the LORD answered me and said: 'Write the vision and make it plain on tablets that he may run who reads it. For the vision is yet for an appointed time; But at the end it will speak, and it will not lie. Though it tarries, wait for it, Because it will surely come, It will not tarry.'"*

3. Count the cost of your vision before starting. Luke 14:28-30 says, *"For which of you, intending to build a tower, does not sit down first and count the cost, whether he has enough to finish it lest, after he has laid the foundation, and is not able to finish, all who see it begin to mock him, saying, 'This man began to build and was not able to finish.'"*

4. Communicate your vision on a regular basis. Know what you want to do and communicate your vision with your partners. You have to know who you are and communicate it a million times before people will know who you are. Talk about your vision with everyone you meet. Put your vision on every piece of publicity you give away. Make sure your vision is on your business card. When people call you, they should hear your vision on your voicemail.

5. Branding is important for ministries. People cannot give to you if they do not know who you are or what you do. However, branding by itself does not raise money. Awareness does not raise money, a vision does. Branding should always be connected with smart fundraising. For example, make sure the end of a publicity video has a fundraising hook; don't just fade off into nothing.

Chapter 5

Communication

Communication is invaluable. As you raise money for your ministry, regularly communicate your vision and your plan. Who are you? What are you trying to accomplish? This continual communication will keep your face and your vision in front of people at all times.

Communicate obsessively with your partners and friends. Remember, it is the squeaky wheel that gets the grease. Out of sight is usually out of mind. Most people are not thinking about you on a regular basis, not because you are not important to them, but because their lives are so busy. Do something to remind them that you exist.

Always talk about your vision. If you don't talk about it, no one else will. You may have the greatest thing in the world going on, but if no one knows what you are doing, how can you sustain it?

Everyone who has given to our ministry in the past year receives a monthly newsletter. Everyone who has given this month also receives an additional thank you letter. People who are on our list but have not given in a long time receive a letter three or four times each year. We also send out postcards and handwritten thank you cards to our top supporters. From time to time, I will call people who have been significant givers.

A large number of people receive an email from me two to three times a month. At the end of the year, everyone who has given will receive an official receipt for their giving. I also send out special mailings to churches to promote my speaking and to bookstores to promote my books. When people mail us prayer requests, we often follow up with a personal call or letter to let them know we are praying.

If this sounds like a lot of communication, you are right. But we view our communication with our partners to be an essential part of our ministry. By writing and calling people, we show that we care, we keep people informed, and we give people the opportunity to continue to support us.

Be prayerful about your communication. Listen to the Holy Spirit. Take time to write your letters so they minister to the needs of your partners. In communicating, remember it's not just about you – it's about your partners as well.

Chapter 6

Persistence

One of my friends sent a fundraising letter to 100 people. He was disappointed that only a couple of people responded to the letter. Because of the lack of response, he decided he was not called to be a minister. He simply gave up too soon.

Winston Churchill was asked to give a speech at a boy's school. After a long introduction by the headmaster, Churchill finally stood up and gave an eight-word speech. He said, "Never, never, never, never, never, never give up." Then he sat back down. This was the best advice that the man whose moral fortitude gave England the strength to resist the Nazi invasion could give.

Once there was a farmer who accidentally left a bucket full of fresh cream in the barn. Two frogs fell into the bucket. They both began swimming, but one frog quickly tired out. He stopped moving his legs and drowned. But the other frog was committed to surviving. He kept kicking his legs until finally he churned the cream into butter. He hopped out and escaped because of his persistence.

Calvin Coolidge said, "Nothing in this world can take the place of persistence. Talent will not; nothing is more common than unsuccessful people with talent. Genius will not; unrewarded genius is almost a proverb. Education will not; the world is full of educated derelicts. Persistence and determination alone are omnipotent. The

slogan 'press on' has solved and always will solve the problems of the human race."

Don't expect any easy solution or magic key for fundraising. Building a ministry takes time, consistency, and a track record. Relationships with partners can only be built over a period of time of being faithful to your calling. Don't be discouraged when money does not immediately come in. Keep doing what God told you to do. Keep telling people what God told you to do. Know you are called by God and trust God for provision. God would not have called you without also calling people to help you. You may have to search hard to find those who are called to help you, but know they are out there.

In *Good to Great*, one of the best business books available, Jim Collins explains what he calls the flywheel principle. I like to call the idea "The Merry-Go-Round Principle." Imagine going to a playground and starting to push the merry-go-round. At first, you strain hard but it moves extremely slowly. As you continue to push, it gains momentum. Eventually the merry-go-round speeds up and you can keep it spinning rapidly with minimal effort. The key to being successful in ministry is to keep pushing the merry-go-round. Any one individual push for raising money may only produce minimal success, but as you continue to push, your momentum continues to build, and over time you will become extremely successful.

Rick Godwin says, "The only thing in life that's easy is quitting; that's why so many people do it." Elisha told Naaman to dip in the river seven times in order to be cured from leprosy. If he had stopped after six dips, he would not have been healed. His persistence brought his miracle.

Start where you are and keep pushing until something works. Billy Joe Daugherty explained how his church was able to build debt-free when he said, "First, we killed the lion, then the bear, and then we killed the giant." Don't try to kill the giant when you have never scared even a kitty cat. Start on the level you are on and build your faith as you overcome obstacles.

Keep on keeping on. Keep pushing until something works. Don't give up. Make steps every day toward what God told you to do. At the end of the year, you will have taken 365 steps towards your dream.

Chapter 7

Education

One preacher said that everything he needs to know is in the Bible. He boasted that he never reads any other book. This attitude is a mistake. Preachers often quote the verse that says, "The wealth of the wicked is stored up for the righteous." Much wisdom about obtaining the world's wealth is found in business books written by successful entrepreneurs.

If you want to be good at raising money, read books about marketing, fundraising, advertising, and branding. Become an authority on non-profit business. Study how museums and hospitals raise money for their projects. Ask questions of people who are experts at fundraising. Attend seminars that teach the principles of philanthropy.

Sign up for mailing lists. How do other people raise money? I started supporting several ministries so I would receive their monthly fundraising letter. (Plus, I believe in sowing seed.) Some organizations pay thousands of dollars to consultants who help them write their appeals. They systematically test their letters by sending them out to a plethora of potential donors. I can see their best material simply by sending them a $10 donation once a month. The better educated you are in the art of raising money, the more you will be able to raise.

Since God will never trust you with resources you are unprepared to handle, educate yourself on how to properly account for money. Ask mentors for advice. By listening to experienced men and women of God, you can avoid mistakes. Proverbs 15:22 says, *"Without counsel, plans go awry, But in the multitude of counselors they are established."*

Marilyn Hickey told me, "Fundraising is a science." There is a right way and a wrong way to raise money. Educate yourself to discover the best ways of raising money.

Chapter 8

Wisdom

One of the most critical tools in fundraising is appropriating the wisdom of God. Proverbs 24:3 tells us, *"Through wisdom a house is built, and by understanding it is established."* Without wisdom as a foundation, anything we build will eventually crumble.

Here are a few keys to keep in mind while applying wisdom to fundraising:

1. Use financial wisdom. Utilize every dollar wisely. What you are faithful with, God will multiply. In the parable of the talents, the master said to his servant, *"…Well done, good and faithful servant; you were faithful over a few things, I will make you ruler over many things…"* (Matthew 25:21).

2. Keep track of every dollar and every donor. Get receipts for everything. Keep detailed records of who gave you money. This information is vital in accounting for your ministry to the government and to your donors.

3. Put aside a percentage of your money for a rainy day. This is hard to do because there is always more ministry that needs to be done than resources available to do it. But if you discipline yourself and put money aside, you will be thankful later. Hard times will come, but if you have money in the bank, you can weather hard times without your ministry failing. I recommend reading *The*

Storehouse Principle by Van Crouch. Proverbs also gives us insight into saving: *"Ants are creatures of little strength, yet they store up their food in the summer"* (Proverbs 30:25 NIV).

4. Negotiate everything. There are two ways to have money: 1) raise lots of money, and 2) spend as little as possible. Remember, the money you raise does not belong to you; it belongs to God. You have an obligation to be a steward with what God has entrusted you. Instead of paying the asking price, always ask for a deal or a discount.

5. Raise money in phases. Do not try to bite off more than you can chew. Put deadlines on what you need. Develop timelines.

6. Be truthful in your fundraising. Do what you tell people you are going to do. The moment you say you are doing something, you had better be doing it, or you are lying. Have integrity in what you do with what people give you. Paul admonishes, *"We want to avoid any criticism of the way we administer this liberal gift. For we are taking pains to do what is right, not only in the eyes of the Lord but also in the eyes of men"* (2 Corinthians 8:20-21 NIV).

7. Know the purpose of money. Larry Keefauver said, "In ministry, money is a means, not an end." Money is simply a tool; it is not a goal. If you focus too much on money, you will lose focus on ministering to people. Jesus said, *"No one can serve two masters; for either he will hate the one and love the other, or else he will be loyal to the one and despise the other. You cannot serve God and mammon"* (Matthew 6:24). Never use ministry money as personal money. Remember, when you receive money for the ministry, it does not belong to you; you are simply a steward over it.

Chapter 9

Variety

We've all heard the cliché, "Variety is the spice of life." In fundraising, variety will add a continued freshness to your efforts. So be creative and think outside the box. God is your source, but He has many resources and ways of getting funds to you. Over my years of ministry, I have tried a thousand different ways of raising money. I keep throwing mud on the walls in order to see what sticks.

As you raise funds for your ministry, try different methods until you discover what works for you. Here are some ideas you might want to try:

1. Write newsletters.

Letters are still one of the best ways to communicate. Sending people a physical envelope in the mail is the best way for people to send you checks.

Jim Zirkle said, "If you expect to hear from your partners on a monthly basis, they had better hear from you on a monthly basis." My parents have mailed out a newsletter to their friends every month for over twenty years. As a child, I spent many long hours stuffing letters into envelopes. My mother would tell me, "Daniel, as long as you are part of this family, you need to help stuff the newsletters." We would frequently stay up all night long working on the newsletter in order to make sure it went out before the end of the month. The consistency of mailing out a letter every single month is what allowed my parents to stay on the mission

field for so many years.

Keys to writing a newsletter:

* Create a good lead-in sentence or question to capture the reader's attention.

* Check grammar and spelling.

* Write in a conversational manner as if you are talking to a friend. Although the letter is mailed out to thousands, it is read by an individual.

* Use the active voice. Avoid passive verbs.

* Keep words, sentences, and paragraphs short. Keep the newsletter simple.

* It is better to say "you" instead of saying "I." Example: Instead of saying, *I was amazed at what God did*, write, *You would have been amazed...*

* Remember, a picture is worth a thousand words.

* Leave some white space. People do not want to read writing that extends from one side of the page to the other side.

* Use underlining to highlight your important points.

* Don't use capital letters unless you want people to think you are shouting.

* Use your newsletter to communicate your vision, to minister to

your partners, and to express your appreciation for their support.

* Put a catch line on the outside of the envelope that will encourage people to open the letter. Since many letters get thrown into the trash unopened, something written on the envelope will sustain a person's attention long enough to open the letter. Handwrite a note if you can.

* Use your newsletters to tell stories about what your ministry is accomplishing with the donor's gift. Also remind the reader that the job is not finished yet and that you still need their help.

* Every letter you send out should include a call to action, a reply form, and a response device (a return envelope). On the reply form, allow the donor to designate a gift to meet a specific need.

* Write from the general to the specific. Begin by sharing what God is doing, then share a need, then ask the reader to help meet the need. Build towards a specific ask at the end of the letter. What do you want the reader to do? Do not ask people to consider supporting you, because all they will do is consider supporting you. Ask them to support you.

* Put together a "Welcome Series" of mailings for new names. When someone gives us his address, we send him three letters. The first letter explains our vision, the second asks for money for a specific project, and the third offers one of our products in exchange for a gift. If he responds to one of these letters, then I put him on our monthly mailing list. However, if he does not respond to my very best letters, it becomes increasingly unlikely that he will ever respond.

  After paying for design work, printing, stuffing, and post-

31

age, it costs us an average of about $1 for every letter we mail out. This means it costs about $12 to put someone on my monthly mailing list. If I mail letters to people who never give, I am simply wasting money.

We mail our monthly letter to everyone who has given to our ministry in the past twelve months. On occasion, we will do a mailing to everyone on our list, just to see if we can turn some of them into regular donors.

Mistakes to avoid when writing newsletters:

* Don't ask for a "one-time gift." It makes it sound like you never want them to give again. Instead, ask for a "special gift" or a "first-time gift."

* Avoid writing about your deficit. Instead, mention specific needs.

* It is best not to ask people to give to your general budget. The giver wants to know more specifically what his gift is being used for.

* Don't ask for finances without giving a time frame for the donor to respond. Give a deadline for raising the money.

* Never apologize for asking for money to meet a need. Remember, you are giving the donor the opportunity to sow into God's work.

2. Write thank you letters.

Whenever you receive a gift, it is appropriate and appreciated to send a thank you letter. When someone gives, we send him a receipt/thank you letter within a few days. People want to know if you received their gift and that you are grateful.

Every month, I write a master thank you letter to the people who give to our ministry. Then, I personalize the first paragraph for the specific giver. This method has proven successful in partner communication.

We can learn how to establish a good rapport with partners by observing the ministry of the Apostle Paul. First of all, Paul regularly thanked his partners in his letters. To his partners at the church in Rome, he wrote, *"First, I thank my God through Jesus Christ for you all, that your faith is spoken of throughout the whole world"* (Romans 1:8). To the Corinthians he said, *"I thank my God always concerning you for the grace of God which was given to you by Christ Jesus"* (1 Corinthians 1:4). He also wrote the following to the Philippian partners: *"I thank my God upon every remembrance of you"* (Philippians 1:3).

Secondly, Paul prayed regularly for his partners. He wrote, *"We give thanks to the God and Father of our Lord Jesus Christ, praying always for you"* (Colossians 1:3). He also said, *"We give thanks to God always for you all, making mention of you in our prayers"* (1 Thessalonians 1:2).

Tips for writing a thank you letter:

* Send a thank you letter promptly after receiving a gift. Mention the amount of their gift.

* Share some recent results from your ministry.

* In every thank you letter, include another envelope. Often people will respond to a thank you letter with another gift.

* From time to time, pick up the telephone and call people who have been faithful givers or who give above a predetermined amount.

3. Send out emails.

I usually send out two or three emails each month. These are short, informative bursts of communication that keep people up-to-date with what we are doing. Emails should be quick, snappy, and frequent. In our modern age, email is how more and more people communicate.

If people do not respond to my letters, we drop them from the monthly newsletter in order to be wise stewards of our resources. However, we never drop anyone from our email list, unless requested. Email is cheap, easy, full-color, and perfect for keeping people informed. It is easy to include pictures and video of what you are doing.

Keys to writing an email:

* Keep emails short, sweet, and to the point.

* Express one idea in each email. People don't have time to read long, rambling emails.

* Use pictures.

* Make it easy for people to unsubscribe from your email list if they want to.

* It is important to have a way for people to have a secure, easy-to-find, and easy-to-use way to donate to your ministry online. People like to give online because of the convenience, speed, and the ability to react quickly to an urgent need.

* Avoid the temptation to email too frequently. If your emails start to feel like spam, you will simply be deleted.

* Build a website for your ministry. Start a blog, use Twitter, You-Tube, and Facebook. In your emails, receipt letters, and newsletters, promote reasons for people to visit your website.

4. Host a banquet.

We host a yearly banquet for our partners in our hometown. This gives us a chance to connect with our friends, give victory reports, and share our goals for the coming year. We usually hold our banquet at a hotel conference room, in a church fellowship hall, or at our own home. Mike Smalley shares these ideas in his book *The Young Evangelist Handbook*.

Keys to hosting a banquet:

* Send invitations to everyone you know in your state. These should include friends from church, people you work with, people you do business with, and anyone to whom you would normally send a Christmas card.

* On the invitation include information about the date, location, and purpose of the banquet. Include an RSVP envelope for people to respond.

* One week before the banquet, call everyone who is attending to remind them of the event. About 10% of those who RSVP will probably not attend, so keep this in mind when ordering food.

* During the banquet, show a video or slideshow, share stories about people whose lives have been impacted by your ministry, and give details about your goals and projects in the coming year. Ask people to partner with your ministry through prayer or monthly support. Also give your guests an opportunity to sow into your ministry by receiving an offering at the banquet.

5. Meet with businessmen.

Terry Henshaw, missions director at Victory Christian Center in Tulsa, Oklahoma, has shared several ideas regarding meeting with businessmen. First, find some businessmen who might be interested in supporting you. Start with the people you do business with, and then look in the paper for companies that donate to big charities. Next, ask businessmen who currently support you to recommend others who might be interested in helping you. Finally, put together a list of potential businessmen, call their offices, and ask to take them out for a meal.

Keys to meeting with a businessman:

* Qualify the person you are asking for money. Research his company. Call his secretary. Ask questions. What kind of charities or organizations does he like to support? How much is he capable of giving? Never ask someone who can only write a $50 check for $50,000 (if you do, you are making his check seem insignificant) or a person who can write a $50,000 for $50 (if you do, you are wasting his time). Also find out what activities he likes. People will display in their office what their interests and hobbies are. Keep your eyes open, observe.

* Invite the businessman to a nice, expensive restaurant. When he is at his office, the phone is ringing, people are asking him questions, and his to-do list is in front of him. The distractions may prevent him from hearing what you have to say. By pulling him out of his environment, you can have his full, undivided attention.

* Before the meeting, go to the restaurant and talk to the waiter. Ask the waiter to greet you by name and tell him to give you the best service you can possibly get. Ask the waiter to make sure your guest's coffee stays hot and his water cup stays full. Promise him

a big tip for giving your guest the best service of his life. The final instruction you give the waiter is that once you pull out your fundraising folder, he is not to bother you again.

* Begin by asking, "How much time do we have?" Because businessmen often have busy schedules, they value their time. Know the amount of time you have with your businessman, and respect his schedule.

* Build a relationship. Show that you care about them personally. Talk about their lives. Ask questions like, "How did your company get started? How did you make your company a success?" Find out what is important to the person you are meeting with. People will sometimes mention their struggles and frustrations during a meeting. Be available to listen to them, and they will appreciate your attentiveness to connection. One big giver said, "All most fundraisers want is my money. I only give to someone who wants a relationship. I don't partner with anyone who does not know the names of my wife and children." Often affluent and wealthy people are looking for someone to speak into their life spiritually. If you will meet their spiritual needs, they will help meet your financial needs. If you will get involved in their life, they will get involved in yours.

* Bring out a folder that details exactly your financial requests. Say, "Listen, I want to share something with you, which is literally life and death for some people. Can you shut off your cell phone for fifteen minutes?" Get your presentation to fifteen minutes or less. Tell the story of what you are going to do. Communicate your passion. Convey that you are going to do the project whether the businessman helps or not. He has to hear the passion in your heart and the commitment in your voice. Remember, you are asking for

other people; you are not asking for yourself. Ask on behalf of the ones to whom you are ministering.

* Invest in making a quality project page to present to business-men. People respond at the level you operate. Present the excellence in your project, and make it look like a million bucks, even if it costs you extra money to print. Do not hand the folder to the businessman until you are ready for him to look at it. He cannot focus on reading and hear you at the same time. Make sure your project page is bullet-pointed. Make it underlined and bold. Show him exactly what you are doing and how much it costs. Business-men are interested in the bottom line. Break the project down into bite-size pieces. Remember, the only way to eat an elephant is one bite at a time.

* Ask the businessman to help with the project. Do not say, "Would you pray about partnering with us?" Most people do not pray, not because they did not intend to, but because they get busy. Once the businessman leaves your meeting, his cell phone will ring and he will likely forget about you.

* At the close of this meeting, simply look him in the eyes, and say, "Would you help me help them?" Don't be shy about this. After you ask, do not say another word until they answer you. If you keep talking, you will talk them out of it.

* Take it to the final step and ask, "Mr. Smith, when do you think I can come by to get that check?" Immediately after you close a deal, send them an email thanking them and reminding them of their agreement.

6. Speak at churches, small groups, and Bible studies.

We take every speaking opportunity we are given, no matter the size of the audience. We find that all exposure is good exposure. When you speak (with the permission of the pastor), attempt to capture the contact information of the people in the audience so you can continue to build a relationship. For more information on how to speak at churches, read at my book *How to Book Speaking Engagements at Churches*.

7. Apply for grants.

There are approximately 100,000 foundations in the United States with almost one trillion dollars in assets. The trick is finding a foundation that is giving money to the types of projects that you are called to do. I only have had limited success in finding grants, but I have some friends who have been far more successful in qualifying for grants. Your success with grants will depend upon how much time you invest in pursuing them.

Tips for applying for grants:
* There are a variety of training programs, consultants, and conferences that will teach you how to apply for grants.

* Applying for grants is a long-term development strategy. Do not get disappointed if you are not immediately successful.

* In a typical grant proposal, include these elements:

Summary: What are you requesting? What is your plan?

Information About Your Organization: What is the calling of your organization? How long have you been in existence? To whom do you minister?

Description of the Problem and Solution: What problem are you trying to solve? Put a face on the problem: Who is fac-

ing this problem? Include persuasive statistics about the problem. What is your solution to the problem?

Your Plan: Describe how you will solve the problem. What is your ultimate goal? What are some specific, measurable objectives for meeting your goal?

Results: How will you measure results?

Budget: Describe your anticipated budget. Include personnel expenses, direct program expenses, and administrative expenses.

Additional Information: You may need to include a copy of your IRS letter granting your ministry non-profit status, a copy of your most recent 990, a list of your board members, a current budget, and general information about your organization.

* Do not try to become something you are not just to win a grant. Many grants are restrictive in nature. Your vision and calling should drive your grant search and application.

8. Develop multiple streams of income.

One of my ministry friends sells real estate, another rents out condominiums, and another is involved with multi-level marketing. A stay-at-home mother helps other ministers promote their books while her husband travels overseas. A part-time job can help pay your expenses while your ministry is starting to grow. But try to give your best and most productive time to the ministry God has called you to do.

We put all our ministry expenses on a credit card that gives us airline miles. Over the course of a year, we earn several free plane tickets. Of course, we pay off the credit card every month or the interest would quickly cost more than the value of any plane tickets we receive.

Chapter 10

Sowing

Several years ago, I had the privilege of meeting Oral Roberts at his condo in California. In the car on the way to his house, I felt impressed by God to sow a seed of $1,000 into his life. At first, I thought I had misheard God. Surely He wanted Oral to give me $1,000! But God was clear, I was the one who was supposed to give.

At the time, $1,000 was a lot of money for me. My brother and I traveled all over America ministering to children through clown shows. We had great fun, but kids give lousy offerings. For several years, we had skimped and saved our money, and we had just enough in our bank account to sow the seed.

Over the years, Oral Roberts has raised over one billion dollars for Christianity. He did not need my $1,000 offering. But God knew that I needed to give it to him. Why? Because I needed a harvest.

In obedience to God, I sowed the seed. Immediately afterwards, miracles began to happen. Before we had received offerings of $4.37, but afterwards we began to receive offerings of thousands of dollars. My $1,000 seed into Oral Roberts Ministry broke the back of poverty in my life.

Another time, I was at a conference with Mike Murdock. On the way to the conference, my car broke down and I left it parked in a person's front yard. After the conference, I was scheduled to do a crusade in Haiti. God told me to sow a seed of $500. I needed the money for my crusade, but out of obedience to God, I gave the offering.

When I arrived in Haiti, I was $500 short of what I needed for the budget. I was upset at God because I did not have the money and my car was dead. We were scheduled to visit two orphanages, but I was so depressed that I did not want to go. I have visited orphanages all over the world, and they all have one thing in common: the director always asks for money to help feed the orphan children. Sure enough, we arrived at the first orphanage and the director explained to me that he needed to buy rice for the children. Our team managed to scrape together enough money to buy six months' worth of rice.

Then we left for the second orphanage. I spotted the director walking toward me and my heart sank. I knew she would ask for money. But to my surprise, she said, "We are so excited you are here to reach our city. We want to help you with the expenses of the crusade." She reached into her pocket and gave me exactly $500, the amount that I needed. It was as if God was saying to me, "Daniel, even in the poorest nation in the western hemisphere, I can provide for your needs."

After I came home, one of my friends called and said, "Daniel, we want to buy you a brand-new car." Because of my $500 seed, God provided for my need and blessed me abundantly.

The funds you need to raise are hidden in a seed you need to sow. You will never have a harvest where you do not sow. If you do not have seed in the ground, you will never grow a harvest.

Once I was praying for God to give me some monthly supporters. God asked me, "Daniel, whom are you supporting on a monthly basis?" I realized that I was not supporting anyone else's ministry on regular basis. I had given larger gifts to people, but I had not developed the consistency of habitual giving. Immediately, I made a commitment to support several ministries on a monthly basis. Within just a few weeks, God gave me more monthly supporters than I had gained in the previous two years.

Mike Murdock says, "The seed you sow determines the harvest you grow. What you do for others, God will do for you." Terry Henshaw says, "The measure of your return is always determined by the magnitude of your sowing."

This is the greatest secret of fundraising I can share with you. If you really want to raise lots of money, then start giving money away. The more you give away, the more God will give to you.

Our Goal?
Every Soul!

Daniel & Jessica King

About the Author

Daniel King and his wife Jessica met in the middle of Africa while they were both on a mission trip. They are in high demand as speakers at churches and conferences all over North America. Their passion, energy, and enthusiasm are enjoyed by audiences everywhere they go.

They are international missionary evangelists who do massive soul-winning festivals in countries around the world. Their passion for the lost has taken them to over fifty nations preaching the gospel to crowds that often exceed 50,000 people.

Daniel was called into the ministry when he was five years old and began to preach when he was six. His parents became missionaries to Mexico when he was ten. When he was fourteen he started a children's ministry that gave him the opportunity to minister in some of America's largest churches while still a teenager.

At the age of fifteen, Daniel read a book where the author encouraged young people to set a goal to earn $1,000,000. Daniel reinterpreted the message and determined to win 1,000,000 people to Christ every year.

Daniel has authored thirteen books including his best sellers *Healing Power*, *The Secret of Obed-Edom*, and *Fire Power*. His book *Welcome to the Kingdom* has been given away to tens of thousands of new believers.

Soul Winning Festivals

When Daniel King was fifteen years old, he set a goal to lead 1,000,000 people to Jesus before his 30th birthday. Instead of trying to become a millionaire, he decided to lead a million "heirs" into the kingdom of God. *"If you belong to Christ then you are heirs"* (Galatians 3:29).

After celebrating the completion of this goal, Daniel & Jessica made it their mission to go for one million souls every year.

This **Quest for Souls** is accomplished through:
* Soul Winning Festivals
* Leadership Training
* Literature Distribution
* Humanitarian Relief

Would you help us lead
people to Jesus by joining
The MillionHeir's Club?

Visit www.kingministries.com to get involved!

THE SECRET OF OBED-EDOM

Unlock the secret to supernatural promotion and a more intimate walk with God. Unleash amazing blessing in your life!

$20.00

MOVE

What is God's will for your life? Learn how to find and fulfill your destiny.

$10.00

POWER OF FASTING

Discover deeper intimacy with God and unleash the answer to your prayers.

$10.00

KING MINISTRIES INTERNATIONAL

TOLL FREE: 1-877-431-4276
PO BOX 701113
TULSA, OK 74170 USA

ORDER ONLINE:
WWW.KINGMINISTRIES.COM

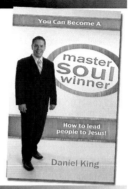
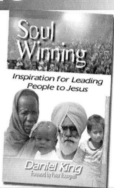

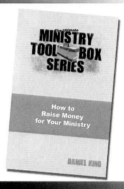

The vision of King Ministries is to lead 1,000,000 people to Jesus every year and to train believers to become leaders.

To contact Daniel & Jessica King:

Write:
King Ministries International
PO Box 701113
Tulsa, OK 74170 USA

King Ministries Canada
PO Box 3401
Morinville, Alberta T8R 1S3 Canada

Call toll-free:
1-877-431-4276

Visit us online:
www.kingministries.com

E-Mail:
daniel@kingministries.com